START HERE, START NOW

Start Here, Start Now

············· **A SHORT GUIDE** ·············
TO MINDFULNESS MEDITATION

Bhante Gunaratana

Wisdom Publications
199 Elm Street
Somerville, MA 02144 USA
wisdomexperience.org

Library of Congress Cataloging-in-Publication Data
Names: Gunaratana, Henepola, 1927– author.
Title: Start here, start now: a short guide to mindfulness meditation /
    Bhante Gunaratana.
Description: Somerville, MA: Wisdom Publications, 2019.
Identifiers: LCCN 2019014015 (print) | ISBN 9781614296270 (pbk.: alk.
    paper)
Subjects: LCSH: Vipaśyanā (Buddhism) | Meditation—Buddhism.
Classification: LCC BQ5630.V5 G87 2019 (print) | LCC BQ5630.V5
    (ebook) | DDC 294.3/4435—dc23
LC record available at https://lccn.loc.gov/2019014015
LC ebook record available at https://lccn.loc.gov/2019980526

ISBN 978-1-61429-627-0   ebook ISBN 978-1-61429-631-7

23 22 21 20 19   5 4 3 2 1

Cover design by Phil Pascuzzo. Interior design by Gopa&Ted2.
Set in Excelsior LT Std 9.25/15.

CONTENTS

one

WHY BOTHER WITH MEDITATION?

Meditation is not easy. It takes time and it takes energy. It also takes grit, determination, and discipline. It requires a host of personal qualities that we normally regard as unpleasant and like to avoid whenever possible. We can sum up all of these qualities in the American word *gumption*. Meditation takes gumption. It is certainly a great deal easier just to sit back and watch TV. So why bother? Why waste all that time and energy when you could be out enjoying yourself? Why? Simple. Because you are human.

And just because of the simple fact that you are human, you find yourself heir to an inherent unsatisfactoriness in life that simply will not go away. You can suppress it from your awareness for a time; you can distract yourself for hours at a stretch, but it always comes back—and usually when you least expect it. All of a sudden, seem-ingly out of the blue, you sit up, take stock, and realize your actual situation in life.

So what is wrong with you? Are you a freak? Are you broken? Are you doing everything wrong? No. You are just human. And you suffer from the same malady that infects every human being. It is a monster inside all of us, and it has many faces: chronic tension, lack of genuine compassion for yourself and others (including the people closest to you), blocked up feelings and emotional deadness—many, many arms.

None of us is entirely free from it. We deny it. We run away from it. We build a whole culture around hiding from it, pretending it is not there, and distracting ourselves with goals, projects, and concerns about status. But it never goes away. It is a constant undercurrent in every thought and every perception, a little voice in the back of the mind that keeps saying, "Not good enough. Not yet. Need to have more. Have to make it better. Have to be better." This is the monster, the monster that manifests everywhere in endless subtle and not-so-subtle forms.

The essence of our experience is change. Change is incessant. Moment by moment life flows by, and it is never the same. Perpetual fluctuation is the essence of the perceptual universe. A thought springs up in your head and half a second later it's gone. In comes another one, and then that is gone too. A sound strikes your ears, and then silence. Open your eyes and the world pours in, blink and it is gone. People come into your life and go. Friends leave, relatives die. Your fortunes go up, and they go down. Sometimes you win, and just as often, you lose. It is incessant: change, change, change; no two moments ever the same.

There is not a thing wrong with this. Change is the nature of the universe. But human culture has taught us some odd responses to this endless flowing. We categorize experiences. We try to stick each perception, every mental change in this endless flow, into one of three mental pigeonholes: it is good, bad, or neutral and not worth attending to. Then, according to which box we stick it in, we perceive with a set of fixed habitual mental responses. If a particular perception has been labeled "good," we try to freeze time right there. We grab onto that particular thought, fondle it, hold it tight, and we try to keep it from escaping. When that does not work, we go all-out in an effort to repeat the experience that caused the thought. Let us call this mental habit "grasping."

Over on the other side of the mind lies the box labeled "bad." When we perceive something "bad," we try to push it away. We try to deny it, reject it, fix it. We try to get rid of it any way we can. We fight against our own experience. We run from pieces of ourselves. Let us call this mental habit "rejecting." Between these two reactions lies the "neutral" box. Here we place the experiences that are neither good nor bad. They are tepid, neutral, uninteresting. We pack experience away in the neutral box so that we can ignore it and thus return our attention to where the action is, namely, our endless round of desire and aversion. So this "neutral" category of experience gets robbed of its fair share of our attention. Let us call this mental habit "ignoring." The direct result of all this lunacy is a perpetual

treadmill race to nowhere, endlessly pounding
after pleasure, endlessly fleeing from pain, and
endlessly ignoring 90 percent of our experience.
Then we wonder why life tastes so flat. In the
final analysis this system does not work.

No matter how hard you pursue pleasure
and success, there are times when you fail. No
matter how fast you flee, there are times when
pain catches up with you. And in between those
times, life is so boring you could scream. Our
minds are full of opinions and criticisms. We
have built walls all around ourselves and are
trapped in the prison of our own likes and dis-
likes. We suffer.

You can't ever get everything you want. It is
impossible. Luckily, there is another option. You
can learn to control your mind, to step outside
of the endless cycle of desire and aversion. You
can learn not to want what you want, to recog-
nize desires but not be controlled by them. This
does not mean that you lie down on the road and
invite everybody to walk all over you. It means
that you continue to live a very normal-looking

life, but live from a whole new viewpoint. You do the things that a person must do, but you are free from that obsessive and compulsive drivenness of your own desires. You want something, but you don't need to chase after it. You fear something, but you don't need to stand there quaking in your boots. This sort of mental cultivation is very difficult. It takes years. But trying to control everything is impossible; the difficult is preferable to the impossible.

You can't make radical changes in the pattern of your life until you begin to see yourself exactly as you are now. As soon as you do that, changes will flow naturally. You don't have to force anything, struggle, or obey rules dictated to you by some authority. It is automatic; you just change. But arriving at that initial insight is quite a task. You have to see who you are and how you are without illusion, judgment, or resistance of any kind. You have to see your place in society and your function as a social being. You have to see your duties and obligations to your fellow human beings, and above all, your responsibility to yourself as an individual living with other individuals. And finally, you have to see all of that clearly as a single unit, an irreducible whole of interrelationship. It sounds complex, but it can occur in a single instant. Mental cultivation through meditation is without rival in helping you achieve this sort of understanding and serene happiness.

Meditation is called the Great Teacher. It is the cleansing crucible fire that works slowly but surely, through understanding. The greater your understanding, the more flexible and tolerant, the more compassionate you can be. You become like a perfect parent or an ideal teacher. You are ready to forgive and forget. You feel love toward others because you understand them, and you understand others because you have understood yourself. You have looked deeply inside and seen self-illusion and your own human failings, seen your own humanity and learned to forgive and to love. When you have learned compassion for yourself, compassion for others is automatic. An accomplished meditator has achieved a profound understanding of life, and he or she inevitably relates to the world with a deep and uncritical love.

Meditation is a lot like cultivating a new land. To make a field out of a forest, first you have to clear the trees and pull out the stumps. Then you till the soil and fertilize it, sow your seed, and harvest your crops. To cultivate your mind, first you have to clear out the various irritants that are in the way—pull them right out by the root so that they won't grow back. Then you fertilize: you pump energy and discipline into the mental soil. Then you sow the seed, and harvest your crops of faith, morality, mindfulness, and wisdom.

The purpose of meditation is personal transformation. The "you" that goes in one side of the meditation experience is not the same "you" that comes out the other side. Meditation changes your character by a process of sensitization, by making you deeply aware of your own thoughts, words, and deeds. Your arrogance evaporates, and your antagonism dries up. And your life smoothes out. Thus meditation, properly performed, prepares you to meet the ups and downs of existence. It reduces your tension, fear, and worry. Restlessness recedes and passion moderates. Things begin to fall into place, and your life becomes a glide instead of a struggle.

All of this happens through understanding.

two

SOME MISCONCEPTIONS
ABOUT MEDITATION

There are a number of common misconceptions about meditation. It is best to deal with these things at once, because they are the sort of preconceptions that can block your progress right from the outset. We are going to take these misconceptions one at a time and dissolve them.

Misconception 1:
Meditation is just a relaxation technique.
Reality: Relaxation is a beneficial byproduct of meditation, but not the goal.

Misconception 2:
Meditation means going into a trance.
Reality: You are not trying to blank out your mind so as to become unconscious, or trying to turn yourself into an emotionless vegetable. If

anything, the reverse is true: you will become more and more attuned to your own emotional changes. You will learn to know yourself with ever greater clarity and precision.

Misconception 3:

Meditation is a mysterious practice that cannot be understood rationally.

Reality: Meditation deals with levels of consciousness that lie deeper than conceptual thought. Therefore, some of the experiences of meditation just won't fit into words. That does not mean, however, that meditation cannot be understood. Meditation needs to be understood by doing it. It is an investigation and an experiment, an adventure every time. Learning to look at each second as if it were the first and only second in the universe is essential.

Misconception 5:

Meditation is dangerous.

Reality: If you take it slow and easy, the development of your practice will occur very naturally. Nothing should be forced. Later, when you are under the close scrutiny and protective wisdom of a competent teacher, you might accelerate your rate of growth by exploring a period of intensive meditation. In the beginning, though, easy does it. Work gently.

Misconception 7:

Meditation is running away from reality.

Reality: Meditation does not insulate you from the pain of life but rather allows you to delve so deeply into life and all its aspects that you pierce the pain barrier and go beyond suffering. Meditation is running straight *into* reality.

Misconception 8:

Meditation is a great way to always feel bliss.

Reality: Meditation does produce lovely blissful feelings *sometimes*—but they are not the purpose, and they don't always occur. Furthermore, if you do meditation with that purpose in mind, they are less likely to occur than if you just meditate for the actual purpose of meditation, which is increased awareness.

Misconception 9: Meditation is selfish.

Reality: The fact is that we are more selfish than we know. The ego has a way of turning the loftiest activities into trash if it is allowed free range. Through meditation, we become aware of ourselves exactly as we are, by waking up to the numerous subtle ways that we act out our own selfishness. Then we truly begin to be genuinely selfless. Cleansing yourself of selfishness is not a selfish activity.

Misconception 10: Meditation means sitting around thinking lofty thoughts.

Reality: Like bliss, lofty thoughts may arise during your practice. They are certainly not to be avoided—but neither are they to be sought. They too are just pleasant side effects. What comes up, comes up. It is very simple.

Misconception 11: Meditation will make all my problems go away.

Reality: Unfortunately, meditation is not a quick cure-all. You may start seeing changes right away, but really profound effects are years down the line. That is just the way the universe is constructed. Nothing worthwhile is achieved overnight. Patience is the key. Patience. If you learn nothing else from meditation, you will learn patience. Patience is essential for any profound change.

three

INTRODUCING MINDFULNESS

This book teaches direct and gradual cultivation of mindfulness or awareness. Traditionally, this kind of practice is known as *vipassana*.

Through the process of mindfulness, we slowly become aware of what we really are, down below the ego image of ourselves. We wake up to what life really is. It is not just a parade of ups and downs, lollipops and smacks on the wrist. Life has a much deeper texture than that if we bother to look, and if we look in the right way.

Mindfulness is a form of mental training that will teach you to experience the world in an entirely new way. You will learn for the first time what is truly happening to you, around you, and within you. It is a process of self-discovery, a participatory investigation in which you observe your own experiences while participating in them. You'll find yourself observing things

17

objectively, exactly as they are—flowing and changing from moment to moment. Life then takes on an unbelievable richness that cannot be described. It has to be experienced.

Through this practice, we train ourselves to see reality exactly as it is. This process of mindfulness is really quite different from what we usually do, tending to see life instead through a screen of thoughts and concepts, which we mistake for reality. We get so caught up in this endless thought-stream that reality flows by unnoticed. We spend our time engrossed in activity, caught up in an eternal pursuit of pleasure and gratification and eternal flight from pain and unpleasantness. We spend all of our energies trying to make ourselves feel better, trying to bury our fears, endlessly seeking security. Meanwhile, the world of real experience flows by untouched and untasted.

In mindfulness meditation we train ourselves to ignore the constant impulses fix, and change, and control—and we dive into reality instead. In so doing, we begin discover real peace. The irony of it is that real peace comes only when you stop chasing it.

When you relax your driving desire for comfort, real fulfillment arises. When you drop your hectic pursuit of gratification, the real beauty of life comes out. When you seek to know reality without illusion, complete with all its pain and danger, real freedom and security will be yours. This is not a doctrine, a dogma, or even a belief; it is an observable reality, something you can and should see for yourself.

Mindfulness meditation teaches us how to scrutinize our own experience with great precision. We learn to watch the arising of thought and perception with a feeling—and our own reactions to stimuli—with calmness and clarity. We begin to see ourselves reacting without getting caught up in the reactions themselves. The obsessive nature of thought slowly dies.

This escape from the obsessive nature of thought produces a whole new view of reality. It is a complete paradigm shift, a total change in the perceptual mechanism. It brings with it the bliss of emancipation from obsessions. Because of these advantages, Buddhism views this way of looking at things as a correct view of life; this is seeing things as they really are.

Included among those things is you yourself: you see yourself exactly as you are. You see your own selfish behavior. You see your own suffering. And you see how you create that suffering. You see how you hurt others. You pierce right through the layer of lies that you normally tell yourself, and you see what is really there.

Seeing things as they are allows you to respond with wisdom.

four

TEN TIPS FOR EFFECTIVE PRACTICE

The following attitudes are essential to success in practice.

TIP 1: Don't expect anything.

Just sit back and see what happens. Treat the whole thing as an experiment. Take an active interest in the test itself, but don't get distracted by your expectations about the results. For that matter, don't be anxious for any result whatsoever. Let the meditation move along at its own speed and in its own direction. Let the meditation teach you. Meditative awareness seeks to see reality exactly as it is. Whether that corresponds to our expectations or not, it does require a temporary suspension of all of our preconceptions and ideas. We must store our images, opinions, and interpretations out of the way for the duration of the session. Otherwise we will stumble over them.

TIP 2: Don't strain.

Don't force anything or make grand, exaggerated efforts. Meditation is not aggressive. There is no place or need for violent striving. Just let your effort be relaxed and steady.

TIP 3: Don't rush.

There is no hurry, so take your time. Settle yourself on a cushion and sit as though you have the whole day. Anything really valuable takes time to develop. Patience, patience, patience.

TIP 4: Don't cling to anything, and don't reject anything.

Let come what comes, and accommodate yourself to that, whatever it is. If good mental images arise, that is fine. If bad mental images arise, that is fine, too. Look on all of it as equal, and make yourself comfortable with whatever happens. Don't fight with what you experience, just observe it all mindfully.

TIP 5: Let go.

Learn to flow with all the changes that come up. Loosen up and relax.

TIP 6: Accept everything that arises.

Accept your feelings, even the ones you wish you did not have. Accept your experiences, even the ones you hate. Don't condemn yourself for having human flaws and failings. Learn to see all the phenomena in the mind as being perfectly natural and understandable. Try to exercise a disinterested acceptance at all times with respect to everything you experience.

TIP 7: Be gentle with yourself.

Be kind to yourself. You may not be perfect, but you are all you've got to work with. The process of becoming who you will be begins first with the total acceptance of who you are.

TIP 8: Investigate yourself.

Question everything. Take nothing for granted. Don't believe anything because it sounds wise and pious and some holy man said it. See for yourself. That does not mean that you should be cynical, impudent, or irreverent. It means you should be empirical. Subject all statements to the actual test of your own experience, and let the results be your guide to truth. Insight meditation evolves out of an inner longing to wake up to what is real and to gain liberating insight into the true structure of existence. The entire practice hinges upon this desire to be awake to the truth. Without it, the practice is superficial.

TIP 9: View all problems as challenges.

Look upon negativities that arise as opportunities to learn and to grow. Don't run from them, condemn yourself, or bury your burden in saintly silence. You have a problem? Great. More grist for the mill. Rejoice, dive in, and investigate.

TIP 10: Don't ponder.

You don't need to figure everything out. Discursive thinking won't free you from the trap. In meditation, the mind is purified naturally by mindfulness, by wordless bare attention. Habitual deliberation is not necessary to eliminate those things that are keeping you in bondage. All that is necessary is a clear, nonconceptual perception of what they are and how they work. That alone is sufficient to dissolve them. Concepts and reasoning don't reach it. Don't think. See.

five

THE PRACTICE ITSELF

Sit upright and allow your body to become motionless, completely still. After sitting motionlessly, close or lower your eyes. Our mind is analogous to a cup of muddy water. The longer you keep a cup of muddy water still, the more the mud settles down and the water will be seen clearly. Similarly, if you keep quiet without moving your body, focusing your entire undivided attention on the object of your meditation, your mind settles down and begins to experience the fruits of meditation.

We should keep our mind in the present moment. The present moment is changing so fast that a casual observer does not seem to notice its existence at all. Every moment is a moment of events and no moment passes by without an event. We cannot notice a moment without noticing events taking place in that moment.

Therefore, the moment we try to pay bare attention to is the present moment. Our mind goes through a series of events like a series of pictures passing through a projector. Some of these pictures are coming from our past experiences and others are our imaginations of things that we plan to do in the future.

The mind can never be focused without a mental object. Therefore we must give our mind an object that is readily available every present moment. One such object is our breath. The mind does not have to make a great effort to find the breath. Every moment the breath is flowing in and out through our nostrils. As our practice of insight meditation is taking place every waking moment, our mind finds it very easy to focus itself on the breath, for it is more conspicuous and constant than any other object.

To begin, take three deep breaths. After taking three deep breaths, breathe normally, letting your breath flow in and out freely, effortlessly, and begin focusing your attention on the rims of your nostrils. Simply notice the feeling of breath going in and out. When one inhalation is complete and before exhaling begins, there is a brief pause. Notice it and notice the beginning of exhaling. When the exhalation is complete, there is another brief pause before inhaling begins. Notice this brief pause, too. This means that there are two brief pauses of breath—one at the end of inhaling and the other at the end of exhaling. These two pauses occur in such a brief moment you may not be aware of their occurrence. But when you are mindful, you can notice them.

Do not verbalize or conceptualize anything. Simply notice the incoming and outgoing breath without saying,"I breathe in," or "I breathe out." When you focus your attention on the breath, ignore any thought, memory, sound, smell, taste, feeling and focus your attention exclusively on the breath, nothing else.

At the beginning, both the inhalations and exhalations are short because the body and mind are not calm and relaxed. Notice the feeling of that short inhaling and short exhaling as they occur without saying, "short inhaling," or "short exhaling." As you continue to notice the feeling of short inhaling and short exhaling, your body and mind become relatively calm. Then your breath becomes long. Notice the feeling of that long breath as it is without saying, "Long breath." Then notice the entire breathing process from the beginning to the end. Subsequently the breath becomes subtle, and the mind and body become calmer than before. Notice this calm and peaceful feeling of your breathing.

The breath serves as that vital reference point from which the mind wanders and is drawn back. That is the frame of reference against which we can view the incessant changes and interruptions that go on all the time as a part of normal thinking.

One traditional simile likens meditation to the process of taming a wild elephant. The procedure for doing such a thing was to tie a newly captured animal to a post with a good strong rope. When you do this, the elephant is not happy. He screams and tramples and pulls against the rope for days. Finally it sinks in that he can't get away, and he settles down. At this point you can begin to feed him and to handle him with some measure of safety.

Eventually you can dispense with the rope and post altogether and train your elephant for various tasks. Now you've got a tamed elephant that can be put to useful work. In this analogy the wild elephant is your wildly active mind, the rope is mindfulness, and the post is your object of meditation, your breathing. The tamed elephant who emerges from this process is a well-trained, concentrated mind that can then be used for the exceedingly tough job of piercing the layers of illusion that obscure reality. Meditation tames the mind.

six

FINDING THE BREATH

The first step in using the breath as an object of meditation is to find it. What you are looking for is the physical, tactile sensation of the air that passes in and out of the nostrils. This is usually just inside the tip of the nose. But the exact spot varies from one person to another, depending on the shape of the nose. To find your own point, take a quick deep breath and notice the point just inside the nose or on the upper lip or wherever you have the most distinct sensation of passing air. Now exhale and notice the sensation at the same point. It is from this point that you will follow the whole passage of breath. Once you have located your own breath point with clarity, don't deviate from that spot. Use this single point in order to keep your attention fixed.

As a meditator, you focus your attention on

that single spot of sensation. From this vantage point, you watch the entire movement of breath with clear and collected attention. Make no attempt to control the breath. This is not a breathing exercise of the sort done in yoga. Focus on the natural and spontaneous movement of the breath. Don't increase the depth of your breath or its sound. Just let the breath move naturally, as if you were asleep. Let go and allow the process to go along at its own rhythm.

Breathing, which seems so mundane and uninteresting at first glance, is actually an enormously complex and fascinating procedure. It is full of delicate variations, if you look. There is inhalation and exhalation, long breath and short breath, deep breath, shallow breath, smooth breath, and ragged breath. These categories combine with one another in subtle and intricate ways. Observe the breath closely. Really study it. You find enormous variations and a constant cycle of repeated patterns. It is like a symphony. Don't observe just the bare outline of the breath. There is more to see here than just an in-breath and an out-breath. Every breath has a beginning, middle, and end. Every inhalation goes through a process of birth, growth, and death, and every exhalation does the same. The depth and speed of your breathing changes according to your emotional state, the thought that flows through your mind, and the sounds you hear. Study these phenomena.

This does not mean, however, that you should be sitting there having little conversations with yourself inside your head: "There is a short ragged breath and there is a deep long one. I wonder what's next?" Simply note the phenomenon and return your attention toward the observation of the sensation of breath. Mental distractions will happen again. But return your attention to your breath again, and again, and again, and again, for as long as it takes.

When you first begin this procedure, expect to face some difficulties. Your mind will wander off constantly, darting around like a bumblebee or a monkey and zooming off on wild tangents. Try not to worry. The monkey-mind phenomenon is well known. It is something that every seasoned meditator has had to practice with. They have pushed through it one way or another, and so can you. When it happens, just discern the fact that you have been thinking, daydreaming, worrying, or whatever. Gently, but firmly, without getting upset or judging yourself for straying, simply return to the simple physical sensation of the breath. Then do it again the next time, and again, and again, and again.

Somewhere in this process, you will come face to face with the sudden and shocking realization that you are completely crazy. Your mind is a shrieking, gibbering madhouse on wheels barreling pell-mell down the hill, utterly out of control and helpless. No problem. You are not crazier than you were yesterday. It has always been this way, and you just never noticed. You are also no crazier than everybody else around you. The only real difference is that you have confronted the situation; they have not. So they still feel relatively comfortable. That does not mean that they are better off. Ignorance may be bliss, but it does not lead to liberation. So don't let this realization unsettle you. It is a milestone actually, a sign of real progress. The very fact that you have looked the problem straight in the eye means that you are on your way up and out of it.

In the wordless observation of the breath, there are two states to be avoided: *thinking* and *sinking*. The thinking mind manifests most clearly as this monkey-mind phenomenon. The sinking mind is almost the reverse. As a general term, *sinking* denotes any dimming of awareness. At its best, it is sort of a mental vacuum in which there is no thought, no observation of the breath, no awareness of anything. It is a gap, a formless mental gray area rather like a dreamless sleep. Sinking mind is a void. Avoid it.

When you find you have fallen into the state of sinking mind, just note the fact and return your attention to the sensation of breathing. Observe the tactile sensation of the in-breath. Feel the touch sensation of the out-breath. Breathe in, breathe out, and watch what happens. When you have been doing that for some time—perhaps weeks or months—you will begin to sense the touch as a physical object. Simply continue the process; breathe in and breathe out. Watch what happens. As your concentration deepens you will have less and less trouble with monkey mind. Your breathing will slow down, and you will track it more and more clearly, with fewer and fewer interruptions.

You may begin to experience a state of great calm in which you enjoy complete freedom from those things we called psychic irritants. No greed, lust, envy, jealousy, or hatred. Agitation goes away. Fear flees. These are beautiful, clear, blissful states of mind—but they are temporary, and they will end when the meditation ends. Yet even these brief experiences will change your life. This is not liberation, but these are stepping-stones on the path that leads in that direction. Do not, however, expect instant bliss. Even these stepping-stones take time, effort, and patience.

The purpose of meditation is not to deal with problems. Don't use your practice to think about your problems. Set them aside very gently. Take a break from all that worrying and planning, from the flurry and scurry. Let your meditation be a complete vacation. Trust yourself, trust your own ability to deal with these issues later, using the energy and freshness of mind that you built up during your meditation. Trust yourself this way and it will actually occur.

Don't set goals for yourself that are too high to reach. Be gentle with yourself. You are trying to follow your own breathing continuously. Take time in small units instead. At the beginning of an inhalation, make the resolve to follow the breath just for the period of that one inhalation. Even this is not so easy, but at least it can be done. Then, at the start of the exhalation, resolve to follow the breath just for that one exhalation, all the way through. You will still fail repeatedly, but keep at it.

Every time you stumble, start over. Take it one breath at a time. This is the level of the game where you can actually win. Stick with it — fresh resolve with every breath cycle, tiny units of time. Observe each breath with care and precision, taking it one split-second on top of another, with fresh resolve piled one on top of the other.

Mindfulness of breathing is a present-moment awareness. When you are doing it properly, you are aware only of what is occurring in the present. You don't look back, and you don't look forward. You forget about the last breath, and you don't anticipate the next one. When the inhalation is just beginning, you don't look ahead to the end of that inhalation. You don't skip forward to the exhalation that is to follow. You stay right there with what is actually taking place. The inhalation is beginning, and that's what you pay attention to; that and nothing else.

Meditation is a process of retraining the mind. The state you are aiming for is one in which you are totally aware of everything that is happening in your own perceptual universe, exactly the way it happens, exactly when it is happening; total, unbroken awareness in present time. This is an incredibly high goal, and not to be reached all at once. It takes practice, so we start small.

We start by becoming totally aware of one small unit of time, just one single inhalation. And, when you succeed, you are on your way to a whole new experience of life.

seven

WHAT TO DO WITH THE BODY

There are traditional postures for meditation, the purpose of which is threefold. First, they provide a stable feeling in the body. This allows you to remove your attention from such issues as balance and muscular fatigue, so that you can center your concentration on the formal object of meditation. Second, they promote physical immobility, which is then reflected by an immobility of mind. This creates a deeply settled and tranquil concentration. Third, they give you the ability to sit for a long period of time without yielding to the meditator's three main "enemies"—pain, muscular tension, and falling asleep.

In choosing one of the postures discussed below, choose the one that allows you to sit the longest without too much pain, and completely

41

without moving. Experiment with different postures. See which works best for you.

The most essential thing is to sit with your back straight. The spine should be erect with the spinal vertebrae held like a stack of coins, one on top of the other. Your head should be held in line with the rest of the spine. All of this is done in a relaxed manner. No stiffness. You are not a wooden soldier, and there is no drill sergeant. There should be no muscular tension involved in keeping the back straight. Sit light and easy. The spine should be like a firm young tree growing out of soft ground. The rest of the body just hangs from it in a loose, relaxed manner.

Your objective is to achieve a posture in which you can sit for the entire meditation period without moving at all. In the beginning, you will probably feel a bit odd to sit with a straight back—but this is essential. This is what is known in physiology as a position of arousal, and with it goes mental alertness. If you slouch, you are inviting drowsiness.

What you sit on is equally important. You are going to need a chair or a cushion, depending on the posture you choose, and the firmness of the seat must be chosen with some care. Too soft a seat can put you right to sleep. Too hard can induce pain.

Traditional Postures

When you are sitting on the floor in the traditional manner, you need a cushion to elevate your spine. Choose one that is relatively firm and at least three inches thick when compressed. Sit close to the front edge of the cushion and let your crossed legs rest on the floor in front of you. If the floor is carpeted, that may be enough to protect your shins and ankles from pressure. If it is not, you will probably need some sort of padding for your legs. A folded blanket will do nicely. Don't sit all the way back on the cushion. This position causes its front edge to press into the underside of your thigh, causing nerves to pinch. The result will be leg pain.

There are a number of ways you can fold your legs.

Native-American style. Your right foot is tucked under the left knee and left foot is tucked under your right knee.

Burmese style. Both your knees and both your ankles touch the floor, cross-legged, with one lower leg in front of the other.

Half-lotus. Both of your knees touch the floor in a cross-legged posture. One leg and foot lie flat along the calf of the other leg.

Full-lotus. Both knees touch the floor, and your legs are crossed at the calf. Your left foot rests on the right thigh, and your right foot rests on the left thigh. Both soles turn upward.

In all these postures, your hands are cupped one on the other, and they rest on your lap with the palms turned upward. The hands lie just below the navel with the bend of each wrist pressed against the thigh. This arm position provides firm bracing for the upper body. Don't tighten your neck or shoulder muscles. Relax your arms. Your diaphragm is relaxed, expanded to maximum fullness. Don't let tension build up in the stomach area. Your chin is up. Your eyes can be open or closed. If you keep them open, lower your gaze or gently fix it downward at a middle distance. You are not looking *at* anything. You are just putting your eyes where there is nothing in particular to see, so that you can forget about vision. Don't strain, don't stiffen, and don't be rigid. Relax; let the body be natural and supple. Let it hang from the erect spine like a rag doll.

Using a Chair

Sitting on the floor may not be feasible for you because of pain or some other reason. No problem! You can always use a chair instead. Pick one that has a level seat, a straight back, and no arms. It is best to sit in such a way that your back does not lean against the back of the chair. The furniture of the seat should not dig into the underside of your thighs. Place your legs side by side, feet flat on the floor. As with the traditional postures, place both hands on your lap, cupped one upon the other. Don't tighten your neck or shoulder muscles, and relax your arms. Your eyes can be open or closed.

In all the above postures, remember your objectives. You want to achieve a state of complete physical stillness, yet you don't want to fall asleep. Recall the analogy of the muddy water. You want to promote a totally settled state of the body, which will engender a corresponding mental settling. There must also be a state of physical alertness, which can induce the kind of mental clarity you seek. So experiment. Your body is a tool for creating desired mental states. Use it judiciously.

Clothing

The clothes you wear for meditation should be loose and soft. If they restrict blood flow or put pressure on nerves, the result will be pain and/or that tingling numbness that we normally refer to as our "legs going to sleep." If you are wearing a belt, loosen it. Don't wear tight pants or pants made of thick material. Long skirts are a good choice for women. Loose pants made of thin or elastic material are fine for anybody. Soft, flowing robes are the traditional garb in Asia, and they come in an enormous variety of styles such as sarongs and kimonos. Take your shoes off, and if your socks are tight and binding, take them off, too.

eight

WHAT TO DO WHEN THE MIND WANDERS

In spite of your concerted effort to keep the mind on your breathing, the mind will likely wander away. As soon as you notice that your mind is not on your object, bring it back mindfully. Following are some suggestions to help you gain the concentration necessary for the practice of mindfulness.

Five Methods of Counting

In a situation like this, counting the breath may help. The purpose of counting is simply to focus the mind on the breath. Once your mind is focused on the breath, give up counting. There are numerous ways of counting. Any counting should be done mentally. Do not make any sound when you count. Following are some of the ways of counting.

In the first method, while breathing in, count "one, one, one, one . . ." until the lungs are full of fresh air. While breathing out, count "two, two, two, two . . ." until the lungs are empty of fresh air. Then, while breathing in again, count "three, three, three, three, three . . ." until the lungs are full again, and while breathing out, count again "four, four, four, four . . ." until the lungs are empty of fresh air. Count up to ten and repeat as many times as necessary to keep the mind focused on the breath.

The second method of counting is counting rapidly up to ten. While counting "one, two, three, four, five, six, seven, eight, nine, and ten," breathe in, and again while counting "one, two, three, four, five, six, seven, eight, nine, and ten," breathe out. This means that with one inhalation you should count up to ten and with one exhalation you should count up to ten. Repeat this way of counting as many times as necessary to focus the mind on the breath.

The third method of counting is to count in succession up to ten. At this time, count "one, two, three, four, five" (only up to five) while inhaling and then count "one, two, three, four, five, six" (up to six) while exhaling. Again, count "one, two, three, four, five, six, seven" (only up to seven) while inhaling. Then count "one, two, three, four, five, six, seven, eight" while exhaling. Count up to nine while inhaling and count up to ten while exhaling. Repeat this way of counting as many times as necessary to focus the mind on the breath.

The fourth method is to take a long breath, then when the lungs are full, mentally count "one" and breathe out completely until the lungs are empty of fresh air. Then count mentally "two." Take a long breath again and count "three" and breathe out completely as before. When the lungs are empty of fresh air, count mentally "four." Count your breath in this manner up to ten. Then count backward from ten to one. Count again from one to ten and then ten to one.

The fifth method is to join inhaling and exhaling. When the lungs are empty of fresh air, count mentally "one." This time you should count both inhalation and exhalation as one. Again inhale, exhale, and mentally count "two." This way of counting should be done only up to five and repeated from five to one. Repeat this method until your breathing becomes refined and quiet.

Remember that you are not supposed to continue your counting all the time. As soon as your mind is locked at the nostril tip where the inhalation and exhalation touch and you begin to feel that your breathing is so refined and quiet that you cannot notice inhalation and exhalation separately, you should give up counting. Counting is used only to train the mind to concentrate on one object.

Four More Tools

Connecting. After inhaling do not wait to notice the brief pause before exhaling but connect the inhaling with exhaling, so you can notice both inhaling and exhaling as one continuous breath.

Fixing. After joining inhaling with exhaling, fix your mind on the point where you feel your inhaling and exhaling breath touching. Inhale and exhale as one single breath moving in and out, touching or rubbing the rims of your nostrils.

Focusing your mind like a carpenter. A carpenter draws a straight line on a board that he wants to cut. Then he cuts the board with his saw along the straight line he drew. He does not look at the teeth of his saw as they move in and out of the board. Rather he focuses his entire attention on the line he drew so he can cut the board straight. Similarly, keep your mind straight on the point

where you feel the breath at the rims of your
nostrils.

Making your mind like a gatekeeper. A gatekeeper does not take into account any detail of
the people entering a house. All he does is notice
people entering the house and leaving the house
through the gate. Similarly, when you concentrate you should not take into account any detail
of your experiences. Simply notice the feeling of
your inhaling and exhaling breath as it goes in
and out right at the rims of your nostrils.

nine

WHERE, WHEN, AND HOW LONG TO SIT

Where to Sit

Find yourself a quiet place, a secluded place, a place where you will be undisturbed. It doesn't have to be some ideal spot in the middle of a forest. That's nearly impossible for most of us, but it should be a place where you feel comfortable, and where you won't be interrupted. It should also be a place where you won't feel on display. You want all of your attention free for meditation, not wasted on worries about how you look to others. Try to pick a spot that is as quiet as possible. It doesn't have to be a soundproof room, but there are certain noises that are highly distracting, and they should be avoided. Music and talking are about the most challenging to work with, since the mind tends to be sucked in by these sounds in an uncontrollable manner.

There are certain traditional aids that you can employ to set the proper mood. A darkened room with a candle is nice. Incense is nice. A little bell to start and end your sessions is nice. These are paraphernalia, though. They provide encouragement to some people, but they are by no means essential to the practice. Many people find a timer, or timing app, helpful.

You will probably find it helpful to sit in the same place each time. A special spot reserved for meditation and nothing else is an aid for most people. You soon come to associate that spot with the tranquility of attention, and that association helps you to reach deep states more quickly. The main thing is to sit in a place that you feel is conducive to your own practice— and that requires a bit of experimentation. Try spots and times until you find one where you feel comfortable.

Many people find it helpful and supportive to sit with a group of other meditators. The discipline of regular practice is essential, and most people find it easier to sit regularly if they are bolstered by a commitment to a group sitting schedule.

When to Sit?

The most important rule here is this: When it comes to sitting practice, the Middle Way applies. Don't overdo it. Don't underdo it. This doesn't mean you just sit whenever the whim strikes you. It means you set up a practice schedule and keep to it with a gentle, patient tenacity. Setting up a schedule acts as an encouragement. If, however, you find that your schedule has ceased to be an encouragement and become a burden, then something is wrong.

So set up a daily pattern that you can live with. Make it reasonable. Make it fit with the rest of your life. And if it starts to feel like you're on an uphill treadmill toward liberation, then change something.

First thing in the morning is a great time to meditate. Your mind is fresh then, before you've gotten yourself buried in responsibilities.

Morning meditation is a fine way to start your day. It tunes you up and gets you ready to deal with things efficiently. You cruise through the rest of the day just a bit more lightly.

Be sure you are thoroughly awake, though. You won't make much progress if you are sitting there nodding off, so get enough sleep. Wash your face, or shower before you begin. You may want to do a bit of exercise beforehand to get the circulation flowing. Do whatever you need to do in order to wake up fully, then sit down to meditate. Do not, however, let yourself get sucked right into the day's activities. It's just too easy to forget to sit. Make meditation the first substantial thing you do in the morning.

The evening is another good time for practice. Your mind is full of all the mental rubbish that you have accumulated during the day, and it is great to get rid of that burden before you sleep. Your meditation will cleanse and rejuvenate your mind. Reestablish your mindfulness, and your sleep will be real sleep.

When you first start meditation, once a day is

enough. If you feel like meditating more, that's fine, but don't overdo it. There's a burnout phenomenon we often see in new meditators. They dive right into the practice fifteen hours a day for a couple of weeks, and then the real world catches up with them. They decide that this meditation business just takes too much time. Too many sacrifices are required. They haven't got time for all of this. Don't fall into that trap. Don't burn yourself out within the first week.

Make haste slowly. Make your effort consistent and steady.

Give yourself time to incorporate the meditation practice into your life, and let your practice grow gradually and gently.

How Long to Sit?

A similar rule applies here: follow the Middle Way, and don't overdo it. Most beginners start with twenty or thirty minutes. As you grow accustomed to the procedure, you can extend your meditation little by little, if you feel inclined. After a year or so of steady practice you might be sitting comfortably for an hour at a time.

You don't need to prove anything to anybody. So don't force yourself to sit with excruciating pain just to be able to say that you sat for an hour. That is a useless exercise in ego. And, again, don't overdo it in the beginning. Know your limitations, and don't condemn yourself for not being able to sit forever.

As a general rule, just determine what is a comfortable length of time for you at this point in your life. Then sit five minutes longer than that. There is no hard and fast rule about length of time for sitting. Even if you have established a firm minimum, there may be days when it is impossible for you to sit that long. That doesn't mean that you should just cancel the whole idea for that day. It's crucial to sit regularly. Even ten minutes of meditation can be very beneficial.

Incidentally, you decide on the length of your session before you meditate. Don't do it while you are meditating, in response to getting agitated, bored, or jittery. It's too easy to give in to restlessness that way, and restlessness is one of the main items that we want to learn to mindfully observe. So choose a realistic length of time, and then stick to it.

Use a timer to measure your session, but resist the impulse to peek at it every two minutes to see how you are doing.

There is no magic length of time. It is best, however, to set yourself a minimum length of time. If you haven't predetermined a minimum, you'll find yourself prone to short sessions. You'll bolt every time something unpleasant comes up or whenever you feel restless. That's no good. These experiences are some of the most profitable a meditator can face, but only if you sit through them.

ten

BARE ATTENTION

When your mind begins to settle, you can set down the techniques described above and move toward bare attention. At some point, you will feel the pleasant sensation of what is called a *sign*. This sign arises differently for different meditators, but it is always associated with the breath, and always has a feeling-tone of pleasantness. Sometimes, this sign is often strongly present at the rims of the nostrils. Unite the mind with this and let the mind flow with every succeeding moment. As you pay bare attention to it, you will see that the sign itself is changing every moment.

Keep your mind with the present moment, this changing moment of the breath. This unity of the mind with the present moment is called *momentary concentration*. As moments are incessantly passing away one after another, the mind keeps pace with them, changing with them, appearing and disappearing with them without clinging to any of them. If we try to stop the mind at one moment, we end up in frustration because the mind cannot be held fast. It must keep up with what is happening in the new moment. As the present moment can be found any moment, every waking moment can be made a concentrated moment.

To unite the mind with the present moment, we must find something happening in that moment. However, you cannot focus your mind on every changing moment without a certain degree of concentration to keep pace with the moment. Once you gain this degree of concentration through practice with the breath, you can use it for focusing your attention on anything you experience—the rising and falling of your abdomen, the rising and falling of the chest area, the rising and falling of any feeling, or the rising and falling of thoughts, emotions, or perceptions.

When you focus this concentrated state of mind on the changes taking place in your mind and body, you will notice that your breath includes the physical part and mental parts. As you notice that, you can notice that both parts are changing all the time. Don't try to create any feeling that is not naturally present in any part of your body. But notice whatever sensation arises in the body. When thought arises, notice that too. When noticing any arising experience, all you need to discern is their impermanent, unsatisfactory, and selfless nature.

This gives rise to an ever-deeper awareness of impermanence, unsatisfactoriness, and selflessness. This knowledge of reality in your experience helps you to foster a more calm, peaceful, and mature attitude toward your life. You will see the subtlety of impermanence and the subtlety of selflessness. This insight will show you the way to peace and happiness, and will give you the wisdom to handle your daily problems in life.

When the mind is united with the breath flowing all the time, we will naturally be able to focus the mind on the present moment. We can notice the feeling arising from contact of breath with the rim of our nostrils. As the earth element of the air that we breathe in and out touches the earth element of our nostrils, the mind feels the flow of air in and out. The warm feeling arises at the nostrils or any other part of the body from the contact of the heat element generated by the breathing process. The feeling of impermanence of breath arises when the earth element of flowing breath touches the nostrils. Although the water element is present in the breath, the mind cannot feel it.

Also, we feel the expansion and contraction of our lungs, abdomen, and lower abdomen, as the fresh air is pumped in and out of the lungs. The expansion and contraction of the abdomen, lower abdomen, and chest are parts of the universal rhythm. Everything in the universe has the same rhythm of expansion and contraction, just like our breath and body. All of them are rising and falling. However, our primary concern is the rising and falling phenomena of the breath and minute parts of our minds and bodies.

Naturally, the mind does not stay all the time with the feeling of breath. It goes to sounds, memories, emotions, perceptions, consciousness, and mental formations as well. When this happens, we simply notice that this has happened, and then we let our mind return to the breath, which is the home base the mind can return to from quick or long journeys to various states of mind and body

Every time the mind returns to the breath, we are actualizing a deeper insight into impermanence, unsatisfactoriness, and selflessness. The mind becomes more insightful from the impartial and unbiased watching of these occurrences. The mind gains insight into the fact that this body, these feelings, the various states of consciousness and numerous mental formations are to be used only for the purpose of gaining deeper insight into the reality of this body-mind complex.

eleven

WALKING MEDITATION

We specifically cultivate awareness through the seated posture, practicing stillness in a quiet place because that's the easiest situation in which to do so. Meditation in motion is harder. Meditation in the midst of fast-paced noisy activity is harder still. And meditation in the midst of intensely personal activities like romance or an argument is the ultimate challenge.

Carrying your meditation into the events of your daily life is not a simple process. That transition point between the end of your meditation session and the beginning of "real life" is a long jump. It's too long for most of us to be able to do without practice. Walking meditation is one way of starting to bridge this gulf.

To do the walking meditation, you need a private place with enough space for at least five to ten paces in a straight line. You are going to be walking back and forth very slowly, and to the eyes of most people you'll look curious and disconnected from everyday life. This is not the sort of exercise you want to perform on the front lawn where you'll attract unnecessary attention. Choose a private place.

The physical directions are simple. Select an unobstructed area and start at one end. Stand for a minute in an attentive position. Your arms can be held in any way that is comfortable, in front, in back, or at your sides. Then while breathing in, lift the heel of one foot. While breathing out, rest that foot on its toes. Again while breathing in, lift that foot, carry it forward and while breathing out, bring the foot down and touch the floor. Repeat this for the other foot. Walk very slowly to the opposite end, stand for one minute, then turn around very slowly, and stand there for another minute before you walk back. Then repeat the process.

Keep your head upright and your neck relaxed. Keep your eyes open to maintain balance, but don't look at anything in particular. Walk naturally. Maintain the slowest pace that is comfortable, and pay no attention to your surroundings. Watch out for tensions building up in the body, and release them as soon as you spot them. Don't make any particular attempt to be graceful. Don't try to look pretty. This is not an athletic exercise or a dance. It is an exercise in awareness. Your objective is to attain total alertness, heightened sensitivity, and a full, unblocked experience of the motion of walking. Put all of your attention on the sensations coming from the feet and legs. Try to register as much information as possible about each foot as it moves. Dive into the pure sensation of walking, and notice every subtle nuance of the movement. Feel each individual muscle as it moves. Experience every tiny change in tactile sensation as the feet press against the floor, and then lift again.

Notice the way these apparently smooth motions are composed of a complex series of tiny jerks. Try to miss nothing. In order to heighten your sensitivity, you can break the movement down into distinct components. Each foot goes through a lift, a swing, and then a down tread.

Each of these components has a beginning, middle, and end. In order to tune yourself in to this series of motions, you can start by making explicit mental notes of each stage.

Make a mental note of "lifting, swinging, coming down, touching floor, pressing," and so on. This is a training procedure to familiarize you with the sequence of motions and to make sure that you don't miss any. As you become more aware of the myriad subtle events going on, you won't have time for words. You will find yourself immersed in a fluid, unbroken awareness of motion. The feet will become your whole universe. If your mind wanders, note the distraction in the usual way, then return your attention to walking. Don't look at your feet while you are doing all of this, and don't walk back and forth watching a mental picture of your feet and legs.

Don't think; just feel. You don't need the concept of feet, and you don't need pictures. Just register the sensations as they flow. In the beginning, you will probably have some difficulties with balance. You are using the leg muscles in a new way, and a learning period is natural. If frustration arises, just note that and let it go.

There is only the sweep of tactile and kinesthetic sensation, an endless and ever-changing flood of raw experience. We are learning here to escape into reality, rather than from it.

Whatever insights we gain are directly applicable to the rest of our notion-filled, motion-filled lives

twelve

THE INEVITABILITY OF PROBLEMS

You will have problems in meditation.

Everybody does.

You can treat them as terrible torments or as challenges to be overcome. If you regard them as burdens, your suffering will only increase. If you regard them as opportunities to learn and to grow, your spiritual prospects are unlimited.

Problems come in all shapes and sizes, and the only thing you can be absolutely certain about is that you will have some. The main trick in dealing with obstacles is to adopt the right attitude. Difficulties are an integral part of your practice. They aren't something to be avoided; they are to be used. They provide invaluable opportunities for learning.

Life is composed of joys and miseries. They go hand in hand. Meditation is no exception.

You will experience good times and bad times, ecstasies and fear.

So don't be surprised when you hit some experience that feels like a brick wall. All seasoned meditators have had their own brick walls. They come up again and again. Just expect them and be ready to cope.

Our job as meditators is to learn to be patient with ourselves, to see ourselves in an unbiased way, complete with all our sorrows and apparent inadequacies. We have to learn to be kind to ourselves. In the long run, avoiding unpleasantness is a very unkind thing to do to yourself. Paradoxically, kindness entails meeting unpleasantness when it arises.

If you are miserable, then you are miserable; that is the reality, that is what is happening, so meet that. Look it square in the eye without flinching. When you are having a bad time, examine that experience, observe it mindfully, study the phenomenon, and learn its mechanics. The way out of a trap is to study the trap itself, learn how it is built. You do this by taking the thing apart piece by piece. The trap can't trap you if it has been taken to pieces. The result is freedom.

Pain exists in the universe; some measure of it is unavoidable. Learning to deal with it is not pessimism, but a very pragmatic form of optimism. How would you deal with the death of your partner? How would you feel if you lost your mother tomorrow? Or your sister or your closest friend? Suppose you lost your job, your savings, and the use of your legs, all on the same day—could you face the prospect of spending the rest of your life in a wheelchair? How are you going to cope with the pain of terminal cancer if you contract it, and how will you deal with your own death when that approaches? You may escape most of these misfortunes, but you won't escape all of them. Most of us lose friends and relatives at some time during our lives; all of us get sick now and then; and all of us will die someday. You can suffer through things like that or you can face them openly—the choice is yours.

Pain is inevitable, suffering is not. Pain and suffering are two different animals. If any of these tragedies strike you in your present state of mind, you will suffer. The habit patterns that presently control your mind will lock you into that suffering, and there will be no escape. A bit of time spent in learning alternatives to those habit patterns is time well invested.

Nobody is telling you to give away every possession or seek out needless pain, but Buddhism does advise you to invest time and energy in learning to deal with unpleasantness, because some pain is unavoidable. When you see a truck bearing down on you, by all means jump out of the way. But spend some time in meditation, too. Learning to deal with discomfort is the only way you'll be ready to handle the truck you didn't see.

Problems will arise in your practice. Some of them will be physical, some will be emotional, and some will be attitudinal. All of them can be confronted and each has its own specific response. All of them are opportunities to free yourself.

thirteen

PHYSICAL PAIN

Nobody likes pain, yet everybody has some at one time or another. It is one of life's most common experiences and is bound to arise in your meditation in one form or another.

Handling pain is a two-stage process. The first step is physical handling. Maybe the pain is an illness of one sort or another or something treatable through medical or other means. In this case, employ standard medical treatments before you sit down to meditate: take your medicine, apply your liniment, complete your stretches—do whatever you ordinarily would do.

Then there are certain pains that are specific to the seated posture. If you never spend much time sitting cross-legged on the floor, there will be an adjustment period. Some discomfort is nearly inevitable. According to where the pain is, there are specific remedies. If the pain is in the leg or knees, check that your pants aren't tight or made of thick material. Check your cushion, too. It should be about three inches in height when compressed. If the pain is around your waist, try loosening your belt. Loosen the waistband of your pants if that is necessary. If you experience pain in your lower back, your posture is probably at fault. Slouching will always hurt your back over time, so straighten up when you notice it. Don't be tight or rigid, but do keep your spine erect. Pain in the neck or upper back has several sources. The first is improper hand position. Your hands should be resting comfortably in your lap. Don't pull them up to your waist. Relax your arms and your neck muscles. Don't let your head droop forward. Keep it up and aligned with the rest of the spine.

After you have made all these various adjustments, you may find you still have some lingering pain. If that is the case, try step two: Make the pain your object of meditation.

Without changing anything, just observe the pain mindfully. When the pain becomes demanding, you will find it pulling your attention off the breath. Don't fight back. Just let your attention slide easily over onto the simple sensation. Go into the pain fully. Don't block the experience. Explore the feeling. Get beyond your avoiding reaction and go into the pure sensations that lie below that.

You will discover that there are two things present. The first is the simple sensation: pain itself. Second is your *resistance to* that sensation. This resistance reaction is partly mental and partly physical. The physical part consists of tensing the muscles in and around the painful area. Relax those muscles. Take them one by one and relax each one very thoroughly. This step alone may diminish the pain significantly. Then go after the mental side of the resistance. Just as you are tensing physically, you are also tensing psychologically. You are clamping down mentally on the sensation of pain, trying to screen it off and reject it from consciousness. The rejection is a wordless "I don't like this feeling" or "Go away!" attitude. It may be very subtle, but it is there—and you can always find it if you really look. Locate it and relax that, too.

That last part is more subtle. There are really no words to describe this inner action precisely. The best way to get a handle on it is by analogy. Examine what you did to those tight muscles and transfer that same action over to the mental sphere; relax the mind in the same way that you relax the body. Buddhism recognizes that body and mind are tightly linked. This is so true that many people will not see this as a two-step procedure. For them to relax the body is to relax the mind and vice versa. These people will experience the entire relaxation, mental and physical, as a single process. In any case, just let go completely until your awareness slows down past that barrier of resistance and relaxes into the pure flowing sensation beneath.

The resistance was a barrier that you yourself erected. It was a gap, a sense of distance between self and others. It was a borderline between "me" and "the pain." Dissolve that barrier, and separation vanishes. You slow down into that sea of surging sensation, and you merge with the pain. You become the pain. You watch its ebb and flow and something surprising happens. It no longer troubles you. Suffering dissipates. Only the pain remains, an experience, nothing more.

The "me" who was being hurt has gone. The result is freedom from pain. This is an incremental process. In the beginning, you can expect to succeed with small pains and be defeated by big ones. Like most of our skills, it grows with practice. The more you practice, the more pain you can handle. Please understand fully: There is no masochism being advocated here. Self-mortification is not the point. This is an exercise in awareness, not in self-torture.

If the pain becomes excruciating, go ahead and move—mindfully—and then resume stillness. Observe your movements. See how it feels to move. Watch what it does to the pain. Watch the pain diminish. Try not to move too much, though. The less you move, the easier it is to remain fully mindful. New meditators sometimes say they have trouble remaining mindful when pain is present—and this difficulty stems from a misunderstanding. These students are conceiving mindfulness as something distinct from the experience of pain. It is not. Mindfulness never exists by itself. It always has some object, and one object is as good as another.

You can be mindful of pain just as you are mindful of breathing. Don't add anything to it, and don't miss any part of it. Don't muddy the pure experience with concepts or pictures or discursive thinking. And keep your awareness right in the present time, right with the pain, so that you won't miss its beginning or its end. Pain not viewed in the clear light of mindfulness gives rise to emotional reactions like fear, anxiety, or anger.

All of that is something added to the sensation itself. You find yourself building a mental image, a picture of the pain, a story of it. You may see a diagram of the leg with the pain outlined in some lovely color. This is very creative and terribly entertaining but not what we want. Those are concepts tacked onto the living reality. Most likely, you will probably find yourself thinking: "I have a pain in my leg." "I" is a concept; "pain" is a concept; "my leg" is a concept. Each is something extra added to the pure experience.

If pain is properly viewed, we have no such

reaction. It will be just sensation, just simple energy. Once you have learned this technique with physical pain, you can then generalize it to the rest of your life. You can use it on any unpleasant sensation. What works on pain will work on anxiety or chronic depression as well.

This technique is one of life's most useful and applicable skills: patience.

fourteen

LEGS FALLING ASLEEP AND OTHER ODD SENSATIONS

It is very common for beginners, and even experienced people, to have their legs fall asleep or go numb during meditation. You may notice that you get very anxious about this, and you have an impulse to get up and move around. Or you may be completely convinced that you will get gangrene from lack of circulation. Numbness in the leg is nothing to worry about. It is caused by nerve pinch, not by lack of circulation. You can't damage the tissues of your legs by sitting. Know this, and relax.

When your legs fall asleep in meditation, just mindfully observe the phenomenon. Examine what it feels like. It may be sort of uncomfortable, but it is not painful unless you tense up. Just stay calm and watch it. It does not matter if your legs go numb and stay that way for the whole period. After you have meditated for some time, that numbness may gradually disappear—or it won't.

People experience all manner of varied phenomena in meditation. Some people get itches. Others feel tingling, deep relaxation, a feeling of lightness, or a floating sensation. You may feel yourself growing or shrinking or rising up in the air. Beginners often get quite excited over such sensations.

As relaxation sets in, the nervous system simply begins to pass sensory signals more efficiently. Large amounts of previously blocked sensory data can pour through, giving rise to all kinds of unique sensations. It does not signify anything in particular. It is just sensation. So simply employ the normal technique.

Watch it come up and watch it pass away. Don't get involved.

fifteen

DROWSINESS, INABILITY TO CONCENTRATE, DULLNESS, AND BOREDOM

It is quite common to experience drowsiness during meditation. After all, you become very calm and relaxed. Unfortunately, we ordinarily experience this lovely state only when we are falling asleep, and we associate it with that process. So naturally, you begin to drift off. When you find this happening, apply your mindfulness to the state of drowsiness itself. Drowsiness has certain definite characteristics. It does certain things to your thought process. Find out what. It has certain bodily feelings associated with it. Locate those.

This inquisitive awareness is the direct opposite of drowsiness, and will generally evaporate it. If it does not, then you should suspect a physical cause of your sleepiness. Search that out and handle it. If you have just eaten a large meal, that could be the cause. It is best to eat lightly if you are about to meditate. Or wait an hour after a big meal. And don't overlook the obvious either. If you have been out hauling bricks all day, you are naturally going to be tired. The same is true if you only got a few hours of sleep the night before. Take care of your body's physical needs. Then meditate.

Do not give in to sleepiness. Stay awake and mindful.

If you are very sleepy, then take a deep breath and hold it as long as you can. Then breathe out slowly. Take another deep breath again, hold it as long as you can, and breathe out slowly. Repeat this exercise until your body warms up and sleepiness fades away.

Then return to your breath.

Additionally, mental dullness can result as an unwanted byproduct of deepening concentration. As your relaxation deepens, muscles loosen and nerve transmissions change. This produces a very calm and light feeling in the body. You feel very still and somewhat divorced from the body.

This is a very pleasant state, and at first your
concentration is quite good, nicely centered on
the breath. As it continues, however, the pleasant
feelings intensify and they distract your attention from the breath. You start to really enjoy
the state and your mindfulness goes way down.
Your attention winds up scattered, drifting list-
lessly through vague clouds of bliss. The result is
a very unmindful state, sort of an ecstatic stupor.
The cure, of course, is mindfulness. Mindfully
observe these phenomena and they will dissi-
pate. When blissful feelings arise, accept them.
There is no need to avoid them, but don't get
wrapped up in them. They are physical feelings,
so treat them as such. Observe feelings as feelings. Observe dullness as dullness. Watch them
rise and watch them pass. Don't get involved.

At the other end of the spectrum, an overactive,
jumping attention is something that everybody
experiences from time to time. It is generally
handled by the techniques to handle distractions presented on pages 49–54. You should also
be informed, however, that there are certain

external factors that contribute to this phenomenon — and these are best handled by simple
adjustments in your schedule.

Mental images are powerful entities. They can
remain in the mind for long periods. All of the
storytelling arts are direct manipulation of such
material, and if the writer has done his job well,
the characters and images presented will have a
powerful and lingering effect on the mind. If you
have been to the best movie of the year, the meditation that follows is going to be full of those
images. If you are halfway through the scariest
horror novel you've ever read, your meditation is
going to be full of monsters. So switch the order
of events. Do your meditation first. Then read or
go to the movies.

Another influential factor is your own emotional state. If there is some real conflict in your
life, that agitation will carry over into meditation. Try to resolve your immediate daily con-
flicts before meditation when you can. Your life
will run more smoothly, and you won't be pon-
dering uselessly in your practice — but don't use
this advice as a way to avoid meditation. Some-

times you can't resolve every issue before you sit. Just go ahead and sit anyway.

Use your meditation to let go of all the ego-centric attitudes that keep you trapped within your own limited viewpoint. Your problems will resolve more easily thereafter. And then there are those days when it seems that the mind will never rest, but you can't locate any apparent cause. Sometimes meditation is like that.

This kind of meditation is primarily an exercise in awareness. Emptying the mind is not as important as being mindful of what the mind is doing. If you are frantic and you can't do a thing to stop it, just observe. It is all you. The result will be one more step forward in your journey of self-exploration.

Above all, don't get frustrated over the nonstop chatter of your mind. That babble is just one more thing to be mindful of.

On the one hand, it is difficult to imagine anything more inherently boring than sitting still for an hour with nothing to do but feel the air going in and out of your nose. Boredom will arise. Boredom is a mental state and should be treated as such. Two simple strategies will help you to cope.

Tactic A: Reestablish true mindfulness. If the breath seems an exceedingly dull thing to observe over and over, you may rest assured of one thing: you have ceased to observe the process with true mindfulness. True mindfulness is never boring. Look again. Don't assume that you know what breath is. Don't take it for granted that you have already seen everything there is to see.

If you do, you are conceptualizing the process rather than observing its living reality. When you are clearly mindful of the breath or of anything else, it is never boring. Mindfulness looks at everything with the eyes of a child, with a sense of wonder. Mindfulness sees every moment as if it were the first and the only moment in the universe. So if all you see is boredom, look again.

Tactic B: Observe your mental state. Look at your state of boredom mindfully. What is boredom? Where is boredom? What does it feel like? What are its mental components? Does it have any physical feeling? What does it do to your thought process? Take a fresh look at boredom, as if you have never experienced that state before.

sixteen

FEAR AND AGITATION

States of fear sometimes arise during meditation for no discernible reason. It is a common phenomenon, and there can be a number of causes. The emotional contents of a thought complex often leak through into your conscious awareness long before the thought itself surfaces. This may be what's happening.

Or you may be dealing directly with the fear that we all fear: fear of the unknown. At some point in your meditation career you will be struck with the seriousness of what you are actually doing. You are tearing down the wall of illusion you have always used to explain life to yourself and to shield yourself from the intense flame of reality. You are about to meet ultimate truth, face to face. That is scary. But it has to be dealt with eventually. Go ahead and dive right in.

A third possibility: the fear that you are feeling may be self-generated. You may be fueling it by fixating on it. In this case, just return your mindful attention to the breath.

No matter what the source of your fear, mindfulness is the cure. Observe the fear just as the arising of fear, exactly as it is. Don't cling to it. Just watch it rising. Study its effect. See how it makes you feel and how it affects your body. When you find yourself in the grip of horror fantasies, simply observe those mindfully. Watch the pictures as pictures. See memories as memories. Observe the emotional reactions that come along and know them for what they are. Stand aside from the process and don't get involved. Treat the whole dynamic as if you were a curious bystander. Most important, don't fight the situation.

Don't try to repress the memories or the feelings or the fantasies. Just step out of the way and let the whole mess bubble up and flow past. It can't hurt you. It is just memory. It is only fantasy. It is nothing but fear.

Restlessness is often a cover-up for some deeper experience taking place in the unconscious. We humans are great at repressing things. Rather than confronting some unpleasant thought we experience, we try to bury it so we won't have to deal with the issue. Unfortunately, we usually don't succeed—at least not fully. We hide the thought, but the mental energy we use to cover it up sits there and boils. The result is that sense of unease that we call agitation or restlessness.

There may be nothing you can put your finger on—but you don't feel at ease, you can't relax. When this uncomfortable state arises in meditation, just observe it. Don't let it rule you. Don't jump up and run off. And don't struggle with it and try to make it go away. Just let it be there and watch it closely. Then the repressed material will eventually surface, and you will find out what you have been worrying about.

The unpleasant experience that you have been trying to avoid could be almost anything. Whatever it is, let it arise and look at it mindfully. If you just sit still and observe your agitation, it will eventually pass. Being able to sit through restlessness is itself a little breakthrough in your meditation career. It will teach you a lot. You will find that agitation is actually rather a superficial mental state. It is inherently ephemeral. It comes and it goes. It has no real grip on you at all.

seventeen

TRYING TOO HARD, EXPECTING TOO MUCH, AND GETTING DISCOURAGED

People of long experience in meditation are often pretty jovial people. They possess one of the most valuable of all human treasures: a sense of humor. They can laugh at their own human failures. They can chuckle at personal crises. Beginners in meditation, on the other hand, are often much too serious for their own good. They are tensed and striving, overly eager for results, taking it all so very, very seriously.

Beginners are often full of enormous and inflated expectations. They jump right in and expect incredible results in no time flat. They push. They tense. They sweat and strain, and it is all so terribly grim and solemn. This state of tension is the antithesis of mindfulness—and so, naturally, they achieve little. Then they decide ·

101

that this meditation is not so exciting after all. It did not give them what they wanted. They chuck it aside.

You learn about meditation only by meditating. You learn what meditation is all about and where it leads only through direct experience of the thing itself. Therefore beginners do not know where they are headed because they have developed little sense of where practice is leading. Newcomers to meditation expect all the wrong things, and those expectations do no good at all.

Trying too hard leads to rigidity and unhappiness, to guilt and self-condemnation. When you are trying too hard, your effort becomes mechanical, and that defeats mindfulness before it even gets started. You are well advised to drop all that.

Drop your expectations and straining. Simply meditate with a steady and balanced effort. Enjoy your meditation and don't load yourself down with sweat and struggles. Let it be simple. Just be mindful.

The meditation itself will take care of the future.

The effect of pushing too hard is frustration. You are in a state of tension. You get nowhere. You realize that you are not making the progress you expected, so you get discouraged. You feel like a failure. It is all a very natural cycle—but a totally avoidable one. Striving after unrealistic expectations is the source

Nonetheless, if you find yourself discouraged, just observe your state of mind clearly. Don't add anything to it. Just watch it. A sense of failure is only another ephemeral emotional reaction. If you get involved, it feeds on your energy and it grows. If you simply stand aside and watch it, it passes away.

If you are discouraged over your perceived failure in meditation, that is, in a sense, especially easy to deal with. You feel you have failed in your practice. You have failed to be mindful. Simply become mindful of that sense of failure. You have just reestablished your mindfulness with that single step. The reason for your sense of failure is nothing but a memory.

Truly, there is no such thing as failure in meditation. There are setbacks and difficulties—but there is no failure unless you give up entirely. Even if you have spent twenty solid years getting nowhere, you can be mindful at any second you choose. It is your decision. Regretting is only one more way of being unmindful. The instant that you realize that you have been unmindful, that realization itself is an act of mindfulness. So continue the process.

Don't get sidetracked by an emotional reaction.

eighteen

RESISTANCE TO MEDITATION

There are times when you won't feel like meditating.

Missing a single practice session is, of course scarcely important—but it very easily becomes a habit. It is wiser to push on through the resistance. Go sit anyway. Observe this feeling of aversion. In most cases it is a passing emotion, a flash in the pan that will evaporate right in front of your eyes. Five minutes after you sit down it is gone. In other cases, it may be due to some sour mood that day, and it lasts longer. Still, it does pass. And it is better to get rid of it in twenty or thirty minutes of meditation than to carry it around with you and let it ruin the rest of your day.

At other times, resistance may be due to some difficulty you are having with the practice itself. You may or may not know what that difficulty is.

If the problem is known, handle it by one of the techniques given in this book. Once the problem is gone, resistance will be gone. If the problem is unknown, then you are going to have to tough it out. Just sit through the resistance and observe it mindfully. It will pass.

If resistance to meditation is a common feature of your practice, then you should suspect some subtle error in your basic attitude. Meditation is not a ritual conducted in a particular posture. It is not a painful exercise, or period of enforced boredom. And it is not a grim, solemn obligation. Instead of habitually viewing it like that, try a new way of seeing it as a form of play. Meditation is your friend. Come to regard it as such, and resistance will disappear like smoke on a summer breeze.

If you try all these possibilities and the resistance remains, then there may be a problem. Certain metaphysical snags that meditators sometimes encounter go beyond the scope of this book. It is not common for new meditators to hit these, but it can happen. Don't give up. Go and get guidance. Seek out qualified teachers of the vipassana style of meditation and ask them to help you resolve the situation. Such people exist for exactly that purpose.

nineteen

MENTAL MANEUVERS FOR DEALING WITH DISTRACTION

At some time, every meditator encounters distractions during practice, and methods are needed to deal with them. An array of practical, traditional meditation maneuvers can help. These techniques can be used singly, or in combinations. Properly employed, they constitute quite an effective arsenal for your battle against the monkey mind.

Maneuver 1: Noticing Distraction. A distraction has pulled you away from the breath, and you suddenly realize that you've been daydreaming. The trick is to pull all the way out of whatever has captured you, to break its hold on you completely so you can go back to the breath with full attention. Just say to yourself, "Okay, I have been distracted for some amount of time," or

". . . since the dog started barking," or ". . . since I started thinking about money." When you first start practicing this technique, you will do it by talking to yourself. Once the habit is well established, you can drop that, and the action becomes wordless and very quick. The whole idea, remember, is to pull out of the distraction and get back to the breath. One way you can pull out of the thought by making it the object of inspection just long enough to glean from it a rough approximation of its duration. The interval itself is not important. Once you are free of the distraction, drop the whole thing and go back to the breath. Do not get hung up on trying to be sure of an "accurate" time-estimate—it really doesn't matter.

Maneuver 2: Deep breaths. When your mind is wild and agitated, you can often reestablish mindfulness with a few quick deep breaths. Pull the air in strongly and let it out the same way. This increases the sensation inside the nostrils and makes it easier to focus. Make a strong act of will and apply some force to your attention.

Allow your full attention to settle nicely back on the breath.

Maneuver 3: Counting. Counting the breaths as they pass is a traditional procedure. Some schools of practice teach this activity as their primary tactic. Vipassana uses it as an auxiliary technique for reestablishing mindfulness and for strengthening concentration. As we discussed earlier on pages 49–51, you can count breaths in a number of different ways. Remember to keep your attention on the breath.

You will probably notice a change after you have done some amount of your counting. The breath slows down, or it becomes very light and refined. This is a physiological signal that concentration has become well established. At this point, the breath is usually so light or so fast and gentle that you can't clearly distinguish the inhalation from the exhalation. They seem to blend into each other. You can then count both of them as a single cycle. Continue your counting process, but only up to a count of five, covering the same five-breath sequence, then start over.

When counting becomes a bother, go on to the next step. Drop the numbers and forget about the concepts of inhalation and exhalation. Just dive right into the pure sensation of breathing. Inhalation blends into exhalation. One breath blends into the next in a never-ending cycle of pure, smooth flow.

Maneuver 4: The In-Out Method. This is an alternative to counting, and it functions in much the same manner. Just direct your attention to the breath and mentally tag each cycle with the words, "*Inhale . . . exhale,*" or "*In . . . out.*"

Continue the process until you no longer need these concepts, and then throw them away.

Maneuver 5: Recalling Your Purpose. There are times when things pop into your mind, apparently at random. Words, phrases, or whole sentences jump up out of the unconscious for no discernible reason. Objects appear. Pictures flash on and off. This is an unsettling experience. Your mind feels like a flag flapping in a stiff wind. It washes back and forth like waves in the ocean. Often, at times like this, it is enough just to clearly recall why you are there.

You can say to yourself, "I'm not sitting here just to waste my time with these thoughts. I'm here to focus my mind on the breath, which is universal and common to all living beings." Sometimes your mind will settle down, even before you complete this recitation. Other times you may have to repeat it several times before you refocus on the breath.

Maneuver 6: Canceling One Thought with Another. Some thoughts just won't go away. We humans are obsessional beings. We tend to lock onto things like sexual fantasies and worries and ambitions. We feed those thought complexes over years of time and give them plenty of exercise by playing with them in every spare moment. Then when we sit down to meditate, we order them to go away and leave us alone. It is scarcely surprising that they don't obey. Persistent thoughts like these require a direct approach, a full-scale frontal attack.

Buddhist psychology has developed a distinct

system of classification. An unskillful thought is one connected with greed, hatred, or delusion. These are the thoughts that the mind most easily builds into obsessions. They are unskillful in the sense that they lead you away from the goal of liberation. Skillful thoughts, on the other hand, are those connected with generosity, compassion, and wisdom. They are skillful in the sense that they may be used as specific remedies for unskillful thoughts, and thus can assist you in moving toward liberation.

You cannot condition liberation. It is not a state built out of thoughts. Nor can you condition the personal qualities that liberation produces. Thoughts of benevolence can produce a *semblance* of benevolence, but it's not the real item. It will break down under pressure. Thoughts of compassion produce only superficial compassion. Therefore, these skillful thoughts will not, in themselves, free you from the trap. They are skillful only if applied as antidotes to the "poison" of unskillful thoughts. Thoughts of generosity can temporarily cancel greed. They kick it under the rug long enough for mindfulness to do its work unhindered. Then, when mindfulness has penetrated to the roots of the ego process, greed evaporates and true generosity arises.

This principle can be used on a day-to-day basis in your own meditation. If a particular sort of obsession is troubling you, you can cancel it out by generating its opposite. Here is an example: If you absolutely hate Charlie, and his scowling face keeps popping into your mind, try directing a stream of love and friendliness toward Charlie, or try contemplating his good qualities. You probably will get rid of the immediate mental image. Then you can get on with the job of meditation.

Sometimes this tactic alone doesn't work. The obsession is simply too strong. In this case you've got to weaken its hold on you somewhat before you can successfully balance it out. Here is where guilt, one of humanity's most misbegotten emotions, finally serves a purpose. Take a good strong look at the emotional response you are trying to get rid of. Actually ponder it. See how it makes you feel. Look at what it is doing to your life, your happiness, your health, and your relationships. Try to see how it makes you appear to others. Look at the way it is hindering your progress toward liberation.

The ancient scriptures urge you to do this very thoroughly indeed. Paradoxically, they advise you to work up the same sense of aversion that you would feel if you were forced to walk around with the carcass of a dead and decaying animal tied around your neck. This step may end the problem all by itself. If it doesn't, then balance out the lingering remainder of the obsession by once again generating its opposite emotion.

Thoughts of greed cover everything connected with desire, from outright avarice for material gain, all the way to a subtle need to be respected as a moral person. Thoughts of hatred run the gamut from pettiness to murderous rage. Delusion covers everything from daydreaming to full-blown hallucinations.

Generosity cancels greed. Benevolence and compassion cancel hatred.

You can find a specific antidote for any troubling thought if you just think about it awhile. But don't get stuck in applying antidotes, know that that is not the end in itself; the real goal is to be able to return to meditation.

twenty

WORKING WITH THOUGHTS, JUDGMENTS, AND SELF-CRITICISM

So there you are, meditating away. You just glide right along following the flow of the breath, in, out, in, out ... calm, serene, and concentrated. Lovely. And then, all of a sudden, something totally different pops into your mind: "I sure wish I had an ice cream cone." That's a distraction, obviously. That's not what you are supposed to be doing. You notice that, and you drag yourself back to the breath, back to the smooth flow, in, out, in ... And then: "Did I ever pay that gas bill?" Another distraction. You notice that one, and you haul yourself back to the breath. In, out, in, out, in ... "That new movie is out. Maybe I can go see it Tuesday night. No, not Tuesday, got too much to do on Wednesday. Thursday's better ..." Another distraction. You pull yourself out of that one, and back you go to the breath, except that you never quite get there, because before you do, that little voice in your head says, "My back is killing me." And on and on it goes, distraction after distraction—but this is what it is all about.

The key is to learn to notice them without being trapped in them. That's what we are here for. Don't think of the arising of such a thought as the enemy; it's just the simple reality. And if you want to change something, the first thing you have to do is to see it the way it is.

When you first sit down to concentrate on the breath, you will be struck by how incredibly busy the mind actually is. It jumps and jibbers. It veers and bucks. It chases itself around in constant circles. It chatters. It thinks. It fantasizes and daydreams. Don't be upset about that. It's natural. When your mind wanders from the subject of meditation, just observe the distraction mindfully.

This brings up a new, major rule for your meditation: When any mental state arises strongly enough to distract you from the object of meditation, switch your attention to the distraction briefly. Make the distraction a temporary object of meditation. Please note the word *temporary*. It's quite important. This not suggesting that you switch horses in midstream, adopting a whole new object of meditation every three seconds. The breath will always remain your primary focus. You switch your attention to the distraction only long enough to notice certain specific things about it. What is it? How strong is it? And how long does it last?

As soon as you have wordlessly answered these questions, you are through with your examination of that distraction, and you return your attention to the breath. These questions are designed to free you from the distraction and give you insight into its nature, not to get you more thoroughly stuck in it.

Asking these questions in response to an arising allows us to divorce ourselves from it, take a mental step back from it, disengage from it, and view it objectively. We must stop thinking the thought or feeling the feeling in order to view it as an object of inspection. This very process is an exercise in *mindfulness,* uninvolved, detached awareness. And then we return to the breath.

The distraction itself can be anything: a sound, a sensation, an emotion, a fantasy, anything at all. Whatever it is, don't try to repress it. Don't try to force it out of your mind. There's no need for that. Just observe it mindfully with bare attention. Examine the distraction wordlessly, and it will pass away by itself. Do not condemn yourself for having been distracted. Distractions are natural. They come and they go. And each time they do, return to the breath.

And: you're going to find yourself condemning anyway. That's natural too. Just observe the process of condemnation as another distraction, and then return to the breath. Watch the sequence of events: *Breathing. Breathing. Distracting thought arising. Frustration arising over the distracting thought. Condemnation arising for being distracted.*

You notice the self-condemnation. You return to the breathing. Breathing. Breathing. It's really a very natural, smooth-flowing cycle. The trick, of course, is patience.

Just observe the distraction and return to the breath. Don't fight with these distracting thoughts. Don't strain or struggle. It's a waste. Every bit of energy that you apply to that resistance goes into the thought complex and makes it all the stronger. So don't try to force such thoughts out of your mind. It's a battle you can never win.

Mindfulness is a function that disarms distractions, in the same way that a munitions expert might defuse a bomb. Weak distractions are disarmed by a single glance. Shine the light of awareness on them and they evaporate. Deep-seated, habitual thought patterns require constant mindfulness repeatedly applied over whatever time period it takes to break their hold. Distractions are really paper tigers. They have no power of their own. They need to be fed constantly, or else they die. If you refuse to feed them by your own fear, anger, and greed, they fade.

The crucial thing is to be mindful of what is occurring, not to control what is occurring. Whatever arises in the mind is viewed as just one more opportunity to cultivate mindfulness. Breath, remember, is an arbitrary focus, and it is used as our primary object of attention. Distractions are used as secondary objects of attention. They are certainly as much a part of reality as breath.

You can be mindful of the breath, or you can be mindful of the distraction. You can be mindful of the fact that your mind is still, and your concentration is strong, or you can be mindful of the fact that your concentration is in ribbons and your mind is in an absolute shambles.

It's all mindfulness.

twenty-one

FIVE FLAVORS OF
HINDRANCE

Distractions come in all sizes, shapes, and flavors. One category of them is traditionally called *hindrances*, because in some sense they block your development of both components of meditation, mindfulness and concentration. But even though we call them hindrances, that doesn't mean they are to be repressed, avoided, or condemned. All we have to do is see them and work with them, in each their five main flavors.

Desire. Let us suppose you have been distracted by some nice experience in meditation. It could be a pleasant fantasy or a thought of pride. It might be a feeling of self-esteem. It might be a thought of love or even the physical sensation of bliss that comes with the meditation experience itself. Whatever it is, what follows is the state of desire—desire to obtain whatever you have been thinking about, or desire to prolong the experience you are having. No matter what its nature, you should handle desire in the following manner.

Notice the thought or sensation as it arises. Notice the mental state of desire that accompanies it as a separate thing. Notice the exact extent or degree of that desire. Then notice how long it lasts and when it finally disappears. When you have done that, return your attention to breathing.

One thing to note, is that craving and desire can also be aimed to things we normally regard as virtuous or noble. You can experience the desire to perfect yourself. You can feel craving for greater virtue. You can even develop an attachment to the bliss of the meditation experience itself. It is a bit hard to detach yourself from such noble feelings. In the end, though, it is just more greed. It is a desire for gratification and a clever way of ignoring the present-moment reality. But the practice even with these noble-seeming desires the name. Notice them, and return to the breath.

Aversion. Suppose that you have been distracted by some negative experience. It could be something you fear or some nagging worry. It might be guilt or depression or pain. Whatever the actual substance of the thought or sensation, you find yourself rejecting or repressing—trying to avoid it, resist it, or deny it. The handling here is essentially the same. Watch the arising of the thought or sensation. Notice the state of rejection that comes with it. Gauge the extent or degree of that rejection. See how long it lasts and when it fades away. Then return your attention to your breath.

Lethargy. This feeling comes in various grades and intensities, ranging from slight drowsiness to utter torpor. We are talking about a mental state here, not a physical one. Sleepiness or physical fatigue is something quite different and, in the Buddhist system of classification, it would be categorized as a physical feeling. Mental lethargy is closely related to aversion in that it is one of the mind's clever little ways of avoiding those issues it finds unpleasant. Lethargy is a sort of turn-off of the mental apparatus, a dulling of sensory and cognitive acuity.

This can be a tough one to deal with, because its presence is directly contrary to the employment of mindfulness. Lethargy is nearly the reverse of mindfulness. Nevertheless, mindfulness is the cure for this hindrance, too, and the handling is the same. Note the state of drowsiness when it arises, and note its extent or degree. Note when it arises, how long it lasts, and when it passes away. The only thing special here is the importance of catching the phenomenon early. If you let it get a start, its growth will probably outpace your mindfulness power. When lethargy wins, the result is the sinking mind, or even sleep.

Restlessness. States of restlessness and worry are expressions of mental agitation. Your mind keeps darting around, refusing to settle on any one thing, with an unsettled feeling is the predominant component. The mind jumps around constantly. The cure for this condition is the same basic sequence. Restlessness imparts a certain feeling to consciousness. You might call it a flavor or texture. Whatever you call it, that unsettled feeling is there as a definable characteristic. Look for it. Once you have spotted it, note how much of it is present. Note when it arises. Watch how long it lasts, and see when it fades away. Then return your attention to the breath.

Doubt. This experience has its own distinct feeling in consciousness. It's the feeling of a person stumbling through a desert and arriving at an unmarked crossroad. Which road should you take? There is no way to tell. So you just stand there vacillating. One of the common forms this takes in meditation is an inner dialogue something like this: "What am I doing just sitting like this? Am I really getting anything out of this at all? Oh! Sure I am. This is good for me. The book said so. No, that is crazy. This is a waste of time. No, I won't give up. I said I was going to do this,

and I am going to do it. Or am I just being stub-
born? I don't know. I just don't know." Don't get
stuck in this trap. It is just another of the mind's
little smoke screens to keep you from actually
becoming aware of what is happening. To handle
doubt, simply become aware of this mental state
of wavering as an object of inspection. Back out
of it and look at it. See how strong it is. See when
it comes and how long it lasts. Then watch it
fade away, and go back to the breathing.

twenty-two

WORK WITH ALL STATES EQUALLY

In some sense, the motiviation to work with the so-called hindrances is easy to come by—after all, it's easy to see them as problematic. Trickier, however, are those really positive mental states that come creeping into your meditation. Happiness, peace, inner contentment, sympathy, and compassion for all beings everywhere. These mental states are so sweet and so benevolent that you can scarcely bear to pry yourself loose from them. Appreciating them, you may feel like a traitor to humanity's suffering. But really, there is no need to feel this way—and we don't need to *reject* these states of mind or to become heartless robots. We merely need to see them for what they are: They are mental states. They come, and they go. They arise, and they pass away. As you continue your meditation, these states will arise more often. The trick is not to become attached to them. Just see each one as it comes up. See what it is, how strong it is, and how long it lasts. Then watch it drift away. It is all just more of the passing show of your own mental universe.

This leads to a general principle for working with all states, one that can seem almost too simple. You want to really see each arising— whether it is pain, bliss, boredom, or anything else—in its natural and unadulterated form. But simply is by no means easy.

The human mind seeks to conceptualize phenomena, and it has developed a host of clever ways to do so. Every simple sensation will trigger a burst of conceptual thinking if you give the mind its way.

Conceptualization is an insidiously clever process. It creeps into your experience, and it simply takes over. When you hear a sound in meditation, pay bare attention to the experience of hearing. That and that only. What is really happening is so utterly simple that we can and do miss it altogether.

Sound waves are striking the ear in a certain

unique pattern. Those waves are being translated into electrical impulses within the brain, and those impulses present a sound pattern to consciousness. That is all. No pictures. No mind movies. No concepts. No interior dialogues about the question. Just sound waves. Reality is elegantly simple and unadorned.

When you hear a sound, be mindful of the process of hearing. Everything else is just added chatter. Drop it. This same rule applies to every sensation, every emotion, every experience you may have. Look closely at your own experience. Dig down through the layers of mental bric-a-brac and see what is really there. You will be amazed how simple it is, and how beautiful.

There are times when a number of sensations may arise at once. You might have a thought of fear, a squeezing in the stomach, an aching back, and an itch on your left earlobe, all at the same time. Don't sit there in a quandary. Don't keep switching back and forth or wondering what to pick. One of them will be strongest. Just open yourself up, and the most insistent of these phenomena will intrude itself and demand your attention. Give it some attention just long enough to see it, then return to your breathing. If another one intrudes itself, let it in. When it is done, return to the breathing.

But don't sit there *looking for* "things to be mindful of." Keep your mindfulness on the breath until something else steps in and pulls your attention away. When you feel that happening, don't fight it. Let your attention flow naturally over to the distraction, and keep it there until the distraction evaporates. Then return to breathing. Don't seek out other physical or mental phenomena. Just return to breathing. Let them come to you.

There will be times when you drift off, of course. Even after long practice you find yourself suddenly waking up, realizing you have been off the track for some while. Don't get discouraged. Realize that you have been off track for such and such a length of time and go back to the breath. There is no need for any negative reaction at all. The very act of realizing that you have been off track is an active awareness. It is an exercise of pure mindfulness all by itself.

In truth, mindfulness grows by the exercise of mindfulness. It is like exercising a muscle. Every time you work it, you pump it up just a little. You make it a little stronger. The very fact that you have felt that wake-up sensation means that you have just improved your mindfulness power.

Apply these principles thoroughly to all of your mental states. This is an utterly ruthless injunction. It is the toughest job that you will ever undertake. You will find yourself relatively willing to apply this technique to certain parts of your experience, and you will find yourself totally unwilling to use it on the other parts.

Mindfulness is an impartial watchfulness. It does not take sides. It does not get hung up in what is perceived. It just perceives. Mindfulness does not get infatuated with the good mental states. It does not try to sidestep the bad mental states. There is no clinging to the pleasant, no fleeing from the unpleasant. Mindfulness treats all experiences equally, all thoughts equally, all feelings equally—all arisings equally. Nothing is suppressed. Nothing is repressed. Mindfulness does not play favorites.

Mindfulness is at one and the same time both bare attention itself and the function of reminding us to pay bare attention if we have ceased to do so. Bare attention is noticing. It reestablishes itself simply by noticing that it has not been present. As soon as you are noticing that you have not been noticing, then by definition you are noticing and then you are back again to paying bare attention.

Carry this into every aspect of your life. After all. the concept of wasted time does not exist for a serious meditator. Little dead spaces during your day can be turned to profit. Every spare moment can be used for meditation. Sitting anxiously in the dentist's office, meditate on your anxiety. Feeling irritated while standing in a line at the bank, meditate on irritation. Bored, twiddling your thumbs at the bus stop, meditate on boredom. Try to stay alert and aware throughout the day. Be mindful of exactly what is taking place right now, even if it is tedious drudgery.

Take advantage of moments when you are alone.

Take advantage of activities that are largely mechanical.

Use every spare second to be mindful.

Use all the moments you can.

twenty-three

THE FINAL FACTOR:
ETHICAL ACTION

There are three integral factors in Buddhist meditation—morality, concentration, and wisdom. These three factors grow together as your practice deepens. Each one influences the other, so you cultivate the three of them at once, not separately. When you have the wisdom to truly understand a situation, compassion toward all parties involved arises naturally—and compassion means that you become more able to restrain yourself from any thought, word, or deed that might harm yourself or others; thus, your behavior is naturally moral. It is only when you don't understand things deeply that you create problems. If you fail to see the consequences of your actions, you will blunder. The person who waits to become totally moral before he begins to meditate is waiting for a situation that will never arise. The ancient sages say this person is like a man waiting for the ocean to become calm so that he can take a bath.

To understand this relationship more fully, let us propose that there are levels of morality. The lowest level is adherence to a set of rules and regulations laid down by somebody else. It could be your favorite prophet. It could be the state, the head of your tribe, or a parent. No matter who generates the rules, all you have to do at this level is know the rules and follow them. A robot can do that. Even a trained chimpanzee could do it, if the rules were simple enough and he were smacked with a stick every time he broke one. This level requires no meditation at all. All you need are the rules and somebody to swing the stick.

The next level of morality consists of obeying the same rules even in the absence of somebody who will smack you. You obey because you have internalized the rules. You smack yourself every time you break one. This level requires a bit of mental control. But if your thought pattern is chaotic, your behavior will be chaotic, too. Mental cultivation reduces mental chaos.

There is a third level of morality, which might better be termed as "ethics." This level is a quantum leap up the scale from the first two levels, a complete shift in orientation. At the level of ethics, a person does not follow hard and fast rules dictated by authority. A person chooses to follow a path dictated by mindfulness, wisdom, and compassion. This level requires real discernment, and an ability to juggle all the factors in every situation to arrive at a unique, creative, and appropriate response each time. Furthermore, the individual making these decisions needs to have dug themself out of a limited personal viewpoint. The person has to see the entire situation from an objective point of view, giving equal weight to his or her own needs and those of others.

In other words, such a person has to be free from greed, hatred, envy, and all the other selfish junk that ordinarily keeps us from seeing the other person's side of the issue. Only then can we possibly discern the precise set of actions that will be truly optimal for that situation. This level of morality absolutely demands meditation, unless you were born a saint. There is no other way to acquire the skill.

Furthermore, the sorting process required at this level is exhausting. If you tried to juggle all those factors in every situation with your conscious mind, you'd overload yourself. The intellect just can't keep that many balls in the air at once. Luckily, a deeper level of consciousness can do this sort of processing with ease.

Meditation can accomplish the sorting process for you.

• • • •

SOME SLOGANS TO
ENCOURAGE MINDFULNESS

No matter how hard you pursue pleasure and
success, there are times when you fail.

. . . .

No matter how fast you flee, there are times
when pain catches up with you.

. . . .

The present moment is changing so fast . . .
that we often do not notice its existence at all.

. . . .

You can only have bliss if you don't chase it.

. . . .

Your own practice can show you the truth.
Your own experience is all that counts.

Nothing worthwhile is achieved overnight.

. . . .

The you that goes in one side of the meditation
experience is not the same you that comes out .
the other side.

. . . .

In meditation, don't expect anything. Just sit
back and see what happens.

. . . .

Don't be anxious for any result whatsoever.

. . . .

Don't strain. Don't force anything or make
grand, exaggerated efforts.

. . . .

Just let your effort be relaxed and steady.

. . . .

It is said that there are only two tragedies in
life: not getting what one wants, and getting it.

There is no pleasure
without some degree of pain.
There is no pain
without some amount of pleasure.

. . . .

Mindfulness is never boring. Look carefully!

. . . .

Let come what comes—and accommodate
yourself to all that you meet, whatever it is.

. . . .

Focus on your own actions—and take responsibility for them.

. . . .

Let go of the habit of clinging to people and
material things—and to our ideas, beliefs, and
opinions.

. . . .

Don't think. See.

. . . .

Pain is inevitable; suffering is not.

Denying your shortcomings and blaming the world for your discontent keeps you mired in unhappiness.

. . . .

The moment you accept responsibility for your situation, you begin to move in a positive direction.

. . . .

The essence of our experience is change. Change is incessant.

. . . .

Moment by moment life flows by — and moment by moment it changes.

. . . .

Let go. Learn to flow with all the changes that come up. Loosen up and relax.

. . . .

Whatever attitudes we habitually use toward ourselves, we will use on others.

You can't ever get everything you want—
luckily, there is another option: You can learn
to work with your mind.

. . . .

Meditation is running into reality.

. . . .

Mindfulness allows you to delve deeply into
life.

. . . .

Accept everything that arises.

. . . .

Accept your feelings, even the ones you wish
you did not have.

. . . .

Accept your experiences, even the ones you
hate.

. . . .

Don't condemn yourself for having human
flaws and failings.

Learn to see all the phenomena in the mind
as being perfectly natural and understandable.

. . . .

Try to exercise a disinterested acceptance
with respect to everything you experience.

. . . .

There is a difference between *watching* the
mind and *controlling* the mind.

. . . .

Watching the mind with a gentle, open attitude
allows the mind to settle down and come to
rest.

. . . .

Trying to *control* the mind, just stirs up more
agitation and suffering.

. . . .

Meditation is participatory observation.

. . . .

What you are looking at responds to the
process of looking.

What you are looking at is you—and what you
see depends on how you look.

. . . .

Be gentle with yourself.

. . . .

Be kind to yourself.

. . . .

You may not be perfect—but you are all you've
got to work with.

. . . .

The process of becoming who you will be
begins first with the total acceptance of who
you are.

. . . .

Ignorance may be bliss—but it does not lead to
liberation.

. . . .

Investigate yourself.

. . . .

Question everything.

Take nothing for granted.

. . . .

Don't believe anything because it sounds wise . . . See for yourself.

. . . .

Moment-to-moment mindfulness helps you avoid regrettable actions.

. . . .

The way out of a trap is to study the trap itself to learn how it is built.

. . . .

Look upon negativities that arise as opportunities to learn and to grow.

. . . .

Rejoice, dive in, and investigate.

. . . .

Dive in, investigate, and rejoice.

. . . .

Meditation takes gumption.

When you are having a bad time, examine that
badness:
observe it mindfully, study the phenomenon,
learn its mechanics.

. . . .

Choose your speech wisely.

. . . .

Avoid overindulgence.

. . . .

Remember to strive for peace with those
around you.

. . . .

Close your eyes for just one minute and you
can experience how a feeling or emotion is
born, grows old, and passes away.

. . . .

The Dharma is shelter we can always rely on if
we simply remember to.

.... • • • • ....

ABOUT THE AUTHOR

 Bhante Henepola Gunaratana, a native of Sri Lanka, is the author of several Wisdom titles: *Mindfulness in Plain English, Eight Mindful Steps to Happiness, Beyond Mindfulness in Plain English, The Four Foundations of Mindfulness in Plain English, Meditation on Perception,* and *Loving-Kindness in Plain English.* A Buddhist monk for more than seventy-five years, he is North America's highest-ranking monk of the Siyam Nikaya sect of Theravada Buddhism. After coming to the United States in 1968, he earned a PhD in philosophy from the American University in Washington, DC. He has led meditation retreats all over Asia, Europe, Australia, and North and South America. In 1982 he founded Bhavana Society

(www.bhavanasociety.org), the forest monastery/
retreat center in West Virginia where he now
lives.

Journey to Mindfulness

The Mindfulness in Plain English Journal

Loving-Kindness in Plain English
The Practice of Metta

The Mindfulness in Plain English Collection

About Wisdom Publications

Wisdom Publications is the leading publisher of classic and contemporary Buddhist books and practical works on mindfulness. To learn more about us or to explore our other books, please visit our website at wisdomexperience.org or contact us at the address below.

Wisdom Publications
199 Elm Street
Somerville, MA 02144 USA

We are a 501(c)(3) organization, and donations in support of our mission are tax deductible.

Wisdom Publications is affiliated with the Foundation for the Preservation of the Mahayana Tradition (FPMT).